PROPERTIES OF MATTER

IT MATTERS

THERESE M. SHEA

PowerKiDS
press™

NEW YORK

Published in 2020 by The Rosen Publishing Group, Inc.
29 East 21st Street, New York, NY 10010

Editor: Jennifer Lombardo
Book Design: Michael Flynn

Photo Credits: Cover, p. 1 Lori Beneteau/Shutterstock.com; (series molecular background) pro500/Shutterstock.com; p. 4 Jakinnboaz/Shutterstock.com; p. 5 Lawrence K. Ho/Los Angeles Times/Getty Images; p. 6 nevodka/Shutterstock.com; p. 7 sondem/Shutterstock.com; p. 9 ESA/Getty Images; p. 10 Gino Santa Maria/Shutterstock.com; p. 11 margouillat photo/Shutterstock.com; p. 12 udaix/Shutterstock.com; p. 13 Imagentle/Shutterstock.com; p. 15 (mountain) Peter Wey/Shutterstock.com; p. 15 (chart) Fouad A. Saad/Shutterstock.com; p. 17 Robert Blouin/Shutterstock.com; p. 19 jultud/Shutterstock.com; p. 20 Albert Russ/Shutterstock.com; p. 21 Nestor Noci/Shutterstock.com; p. 22 Africa Studio/Shutterstock.com; p. 23 Science & Society Picture Library/SSPL/Getty Images; p. 25 Everett Historical/Shutterstock.com; p. 26 Jamie Hooper/Shutterstock.com; p. 27 SHONE/Gamma-Rapho/Getty Images; p. 29 antoniodiaz/Shutterstock.com; p. 30 PhotostockAR/Shutterstock.com.

Cataloging-in-Publication Data

Names: Shea, Therese.
Title: Properties of matter: it matters / Therese Shea.
Description: New York : PowerKids Press, 2020. | Series: Spotlight on physical science | Includes glossary and index.
Identifiers: ISBN 9781725313347 (pbk.) | ISBN 9781725313378 (library bound) | ISBN 9781725313354 (6 pack)
Subjects: LCSH: Matter--Juvenile literature. | Matter--Properties--Juvenile literature.
Classification: LCC QC173.16 S43 2020 | DDC 530.4--dc23

Manufactured in the United States of America

CPSIA Compliance Information: Batch #CWPK20. For further information contact Rosen Publishing, New York, New York at 1-800-237-9932.

CONTENTS

CHAPTER ONE

WHAT'S THE MATTER?

Matter is anything that takes up space. That includes everything around us, even things we can't see or feel. These are all made up of atoms, and atoms combine with other atoms to form molecules.

STATES OF MATTER

 SOLID

LIQUID

GAS

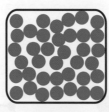

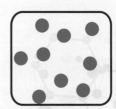

SOLID
STATE

LIQUID
STATE

GAS
STATE

On Earth, we only see the form of matter called plasma in glowing neon signs, lightning, and a few other places. This device in a University of California, Los Angeles, lab produces plasma!

On Earth, matter generally comes in the forms of solids, liquids, and gases. Matter can change forms. Water changes from ice to liquid water and then to water vapor as increasing temperatures break down the bonds between molecules. There are several other forms of matter, including plasma. These aren't generally found in nature, but scientists have created them in labs.

All forms of matter have certain properties that scientists use when they talk and write about them, group them, and learn how best to use them in products we need, medicines we take, and machines we use. All properties of matter have to do with the physical or chemical state of a **substance**.

CHAPTER TWO

USE YOUR SENSES

The physical properties of matter are the ones that can be seen or measured without changing the matter itself. Color is a physical property of matter. It's easily observed. However, the colors of things can change without the matter changing. You can paint the walls of your bedroom or dye your hair. The walls and your hair remain the same matter, though. Changing color does sometimes indicate a chemical change. The changing color of leaves tells us that chlorophyll, a chemical that gives leaves their green color, is breaking down. Other chemicals are at work in the leaves, turning them different colors.

Texture is another physical property of matter. Like color, texture can change. For example, wood can feel rough until it's smoothed with sandpaper. The matter of the wood is unchanged, however.

Smell is a physical property of matter, too. Not all substances have a noticeable smell. That's why natural gas companies add sulfur, which smells like rotting eggs, to the odorless, invisible gas often used to heat ovens and run other household **appliances**. If they didn't, you wouldn't be able to tell if there was a gas leak.

CHAPTER THREE

MASS VS. WEIGHT

Two more physical properties of matter are mass and weight. Some people think these properties are the same, but they aren't. Mass is the amount of matter in an object. Weight is a measurement of the downward pull of gravity on an object. What's the difference? Mass doesn't change, but weight can change depending on your location. The pull of gravity if you're on the moon is less than the pull of gravity if you're on Earth, because the moon's mass is so much less. So you weigh less on the moon, but you still have the same mass—or the same amount of matter in you—in both places.

Despite this difference, most people measure both weight and mass in ounces or pounds in the United States and grams and kilograms in most other countries. Scientists also generally measure mass in grams and kilograms, but they use units of force called newtons to measure weight.

On the International Space Station, astronauts don't weigh as much as they do on Earth. Their mass is the same, though!

CHAPTER FOUR

MEASURING VOLUME

The amount of space that matter takes up is called volume, another physical property of matter. It's measured differently depending on the matter's state, or whether a substance is a solid, liquid, or gas.

A liquid's volume can be measured in a measuring cup or a special container called a graduated **cylinder**. The volume of something solid is measured according to its shape. For example, a rectangular block's volume can be found by multiplying its length times its width times its height. The volume of a gas changes depending on its container! That's because gases expand in whatever container they're in. The larger the container, the more the molecules that make up the gases spread out.

Scientists often use units called cubic centimeters to measure volume. When you buy milk or juice at a store, you may see units called gallons, liters, or ounces on their containers.

GRADUATED CYLINDER

Measuring volume correctly is important when you're cooking—or doing science experiments.

CHAPTER FIVE

HOW DENSE?

Density—or the amount of matter that fits in a space—is another physical property of matter. Objects with high density have atoms or molecules packed very closely together. Objects with a lower density aren't packed as tightly.

It's not easy to see an object's density by looking at it. However, density helps explain things we observe in everyday life. Ice is harder than liquid water, but it's not as dense. That's why ice cubes float. Measuring the density of different building materials is important for engineers who are designing vehicles that float or fly.

DENSITY OF GASES

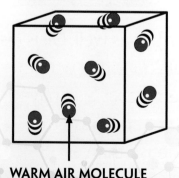

WARM AIR

WARM AIR MOLECULE

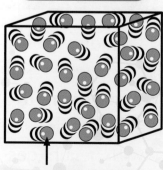

COLD AIR

COLD AIR MOLECULE

Hot-air balloons fly because heated air within the balloon is less dense than the cool air around it.

Liquids can have different densities as well. Oil is less dense than water. That's why oil floats on top of water. Although it's hard to observe, different gases also have different densities. Helium balloons float because they're filled with helium gas, which is less dense than air.

CHAPTER SIX

BOILING AND FREEZING POINTS

The boiling point of a liquid, or the temperature at which it boils, is another physical property of matter. The stronger the attraction between molecules and atoms in the matter, the higher the boiling point. You probably know that you can heat water until it boils. The boiling point of water is 212°Fahrenheit (100°Celsius) at sea level. At the boiling point, molecules in the liquid freely break away and form a gas.

The freezing point of a liquid is the temperature at which it becomes a solid. The removal of heat means the molecules of the liquid draw closer together. Water freezes into ice at 32°F (0°C) at sea level.

Different liquids have different freezing and boiling points. Scientists may add chemicals to **solutions** to change these points so the liquids don't freeze in winter weather or boil in hot conditions.

As this picture shows, the higher the altitude, the lower the boiling point of water is. That's because there's less atmospheric pressure acting on the water. Similarly, the higher the pressure, the lower the freezing temperature.

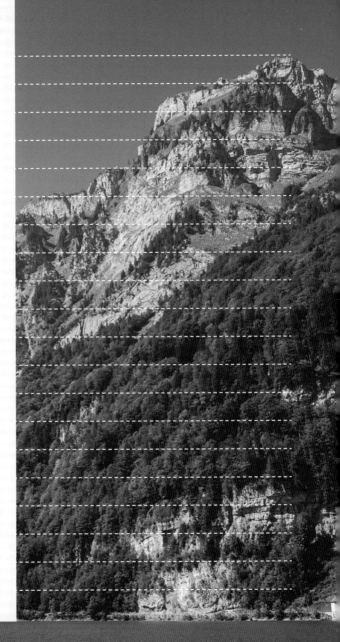

ALTITUDE		BOILING POINT	
(ft)	*(m)*	*(°F)*	*(°C)*
10000	3048	193.2	89.6
9500	2896	194.1	90.1
9000	2743	195.0	90.6
8500	2591	196.0	91.1
8000	2438	196.9	91.6
7500	2286	197.8	92.1
7000	2134	198.7	92.6
6500	1981	199.6	93.1
6000	1829	200.6	93.6
5500	1676	201.5	94.2
5000	1524	202.4	94.7
4500	1372	203.4	95.2
4000	1219	204.3	95.7
3500	1067	205.3	96.3
3000	914	206.2	96.8
2500	762	207.2	97.3
2000	610	208.1	97.8
1500	457	209.1	98.4
1000	305	210.1	98.9
500	152	211.0	99.5
0	0	212.0	100.0

CHAPTER SEVEN

CAN IT CONDUCT?

The physical property called conductivity is the ability to move heat or electricity from one place to another. Materials that can move heat are said to have thermal conductivity. Metals with high thermal conductivity, such as copper, are used for kitchen saucepans. Copper can conduct heat from the stove to the food within the pan. Diamonds also have high thermal conductivity. They're sometimes used to conduct heat within computers and electronic devices, keeping other parts from overheating.

Another kind of conductivity is electrical conductivity, or the ability to carry an electric current. Examples of good electrical conductors are silver, copper, and gold. Almost all electrical wires are made from one of these metals. Materials called insulators are those with poor or no electrical conductivity. These include plastics and rubber. They're sometimes used as covering for electrical wires as well as the handles of kitchen pans.

Electrical workers wear gloves made completely of rubber when fixing power lines. Rubber is an insulator that keeps workers from getting seriously injured by electricity.

CHAPTER EIGHT

MAGNETS MOVE

An object's magnetism, or its ability to be attracted by a magnet, is another physical property. Some objects are permanent magnets—they're always magnetic. Other substances become magnetic because of the effects of other magnets. The most magnetic metals are iron, nickel, and cobalt. In 2010, Jian-Ping Wang and his team of scientists at the University of Minnesota created a **compound** of iron and nitrogen which is now thought to be the most magnetic substance on Earth. However, all kinds of matter—even wood, air, and water—take on magnetic properties when placed in a **magnetic field**. The force of magnetism is so weak that the effects aren't easily observed, though.

Magnetic fields push and pull electrons. That's why magnets can be used for the production and transmission of electric currents, which contain electrons. Magnetism and electricity are closely linked.

An electromagnet uses an electric current and magnetic matter to create a strong magnetic field. Electromagnets are found in countless machines and electronics, including computers.

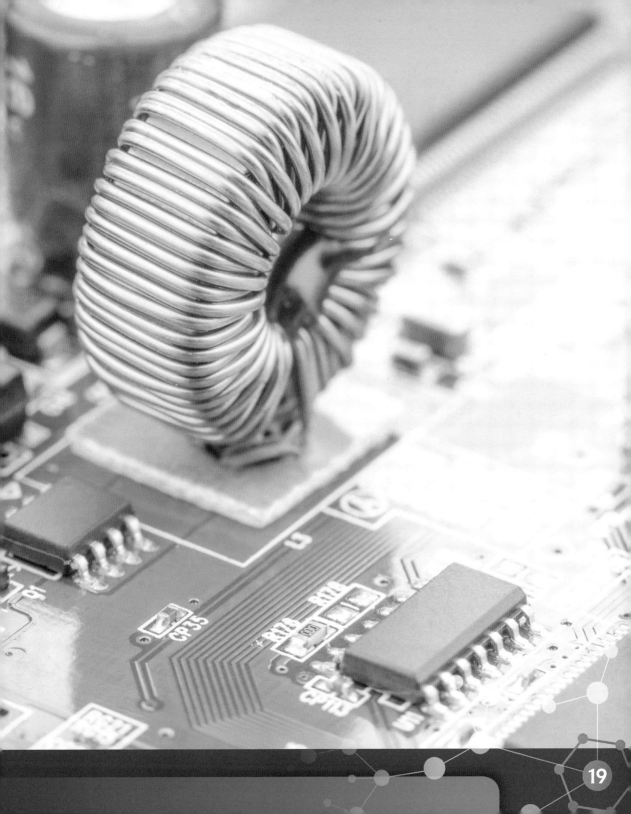

CHAPTER NINE

IS IT REACTIVE?

While physical properties are qualities that can be observed without changing matter, chemical properties can only be observed by changing the structure of the matter until it's another kind of matter. This often happens as the result of a chemical reaction.

One chemical property is reactivity, or the ability of a matter to combine with other matter chemically. Some kinds of matter are very reactive. For example, potassium is so reactive that it's not found as a pure element in nature. When potassium combines with water, it explodes, creating heat and hydrogen gas. Iron is highly reactive with oxygen. The chemical reaction between iron and oxygen creates iron oxide, or rust. There are ways to avoid rust and preserve the strength of iron, such as creating an iron **alloy** called stainless steel, which contains the rust-resistant element chromium.

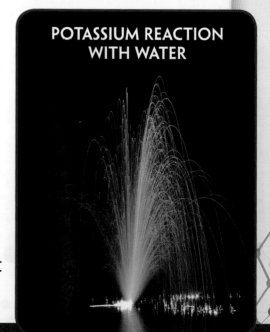

POTASSIUM REACTION WITH WATER

The Statue of Liberty is green because of a chemical reaction. The statue is covered with copper. When this element reacts with air, it forms a protective layer: the green color we see today.

While some substances are highly reactive, others aren't reactive at all. For example, the noble gases are known for being highly unreactive. These are helium, neon, argon, krypton, xenon, and radon. Sometimes they're called "inert," a word which means "inactive."

HELIUM-FILLED BALLOONS

Scientists have explained why these elements don't react easily with other substances. Basically, they're stable because of the arrangement of the eight electrons on the outside of their atoms. These atoms don't lose or gain electrons—a process that would lead to chemical reactions.

Substances' unreactive chemical properties are useful for many situations. For example, argon is used in some light bulbs because it doesn't react with metals at high temperatures as another gas might. The noble gases are also sometimes used to make other substances more stable during chemical reactions.

Between 1894 and 1910, Sir William Ramsay discovered the gases neon, argon, krypton, and xenon. Along with helium and radon, these elements make up the group called noble gases. Here, Ramsay is shown in his laboratory around 1900.

CHAPTER TEN

DOES IT BURN?

Flammability is the ability of matter to burn, and it's another chemical property. When substances burn, they're undergoing a chemical reaction. This means they become an entirely new substance. When something burns, the atoms or molecules of the substance are combining with oxygen and releasing energy in the form of heat and light. The scientific word for burning is combustion. Combustion begins with high temperatures.

For example, wood is highly flammable. When a heat source starts a fire, the wood will burn as it combines with oxygen, changing into ashes. The flammability of matter such as coal supplies heat and power. When the highly flammable element hydrogen burns, it combines with oxygen to create light, heat, and water. Knowing if a substance is flammable or nonflammable is often an important part of staying safe. Sometimes it can even be a matter of life or death.

The airship called the *Hindenburg* burst into flames in 1937, killing 35 of the 97 people on board. It was filled with hydrogen gas, which is highly flammable.

CHAPTER ELEVEN

TOXIC TALK

The chemical property called toxicity has to do with the ability of matter to poison living things. For example, certain elements, such as radium and plutonium, have a high toxicity and can cause **cancer** in humans. By knowing a substance's toxicity, people can learn how to safely use it if they need to.

In 1986, an accident caused a nuclear power plant in Chernobyl, Ukraine (shown here), to spread radiation all over the city. Many people died, and there's still some radiation left there today.

Not all substances are equally toxic to all living things. For example, a chemical in chocolate called theobromine can be toxic to dogs but isn't generally harmful to people. Also, some substances aren't toxic unless they're touched, eaten, **inhaled**, or taken into the body in some other way. However, some **radioactive** elements can harm people without being touched. Harmful particles from these elements can travel through the air, enter the human body, and damage cells. That's why people who live near nuclear power plants are **evacuated** when radiation is released following an accident.

CHAPTER TWELVE

WHAT IS SOLUBILITY?

Solubility is the property of matter that relates to how well a material can be dissolved, or broken down and absorbed in liquid. Salt, for example, is easily dissolved by water. It's soluble. Sand, however, doesn't dissolve in water. It's insoluble. Solubility is an important property in many medicines. Our bodies can absorb medicines that are soluble in water.

Whether solubility is a chemical or physical property depends on the situation. If something dissolves without the chemical bonds between its molecules breaking, it's just undergoing a physical change, not a chemical one. For example, sugar doesn't lose its chemical identity in water. However, if the substance dissolves and breaks its chemical bonds, it undergoes a chemical change—a change in the structure of its matter. In that case, solubility would be a chemical property.

If too much soluble matter is added to a liquid, it may not dissolve. This is important to know when adding sugar to lemonade. Don't add too much!

CHAPTER THIRTEEN

NEED-TO-KNOW INFO

There are many more properties of matter, both physical and chemical. Knowing about a substance's physical properties is important because it helps us predict if it's the best substance for a particular use. Knowing a substance's chemical properties helps us know how it will react in a particular situation. For example, chemical reactions make it possible to take unhealthy substances out of water so it's safe to drink. This process is called purifying.

Future scientists can start using their observation skills to gather information about a substance's physical and chemical properties. They can observe and measure to make lists of physical properties. They can watch for signs of chemical reactions, such as fizzing, bubbles, and even sudden smells. There are a lot of clues to gather about the nature of matter! Are you ready to be a science detective?

GLOSSARY

alloy (AA-loy) Matter made of two or more metals, or a metal and a nonmetal, melted together.

appliance (uh-PLY-uhns) A device designed for a particular use.

cancer (KAN-suhr) A disease caused by the uncontrolled growth of cells in the body.

compound (KAHM-pownd) A substance created when the atoms of two or more chemical elements join together.

cylinder (SIH-luhn-duhr) A solid object shaped like a tube.

evacuate (ih-VAA-kyuh-wayt) To withdraw from a place for protection.

inhale (in-HALE) To breathe in.

magnetic field (mag-NEH-tihk FEELD) The area around a magnet where its pull is felt. Earth has a magnetic field, too.

radioactive (ray-dee-oh-AK-tihv) Putting out harmful energy in the form of tiny particles.

solution (suh-LOO-shuhn) A liquid in which something has been dissolved.

substance (SUHB-stuhns) A material of any kind.

texture (TEKS-churhr) The structure, feel, and appearance of something.

INDEX

PRIMARY SOURCE LIST

Page 23
Sir William Ramsay in his lab in London, England. Photograph. c. 1900. Getty Images.

Page 25
The *Hindenburg* on fire in Lakehurst, New Jersey. Photograph. May 6, 1937. Sam Shere. Wikimedia Commons.

Page 27
Chernobyl nuclear power plant three days after the explosion. Photograph. April 29, 1986. Getty Images.

WEBSITES

Due to the changing nature of Internet links, PowerKids Press has developed an online list of websites related to the subject of this book. This site is updated regularly. Please use this link to access the list: www.powerkidslinks.com/SOPS/matter